T0199042

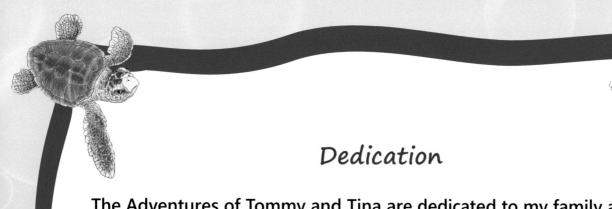

Dedication

The Adventures of Tommy and Tina are dedicated to my family and my many friends who have given me many great memories of fun times that we have spent together.

AUTHOR

Rod Burns is an Author of Educational and Fun Stories for all ages and lives on the Treasure Coast.

To order additional copies of this book, contact:
Xlibris
844-714-8691
www.Xlibris.com
Orders@Xlibris.com

ILLUSTRATOR
Jay Fairchild

ISBN: Softcover   978-1-6641-4664-8
       EBook   978-1-6641-4663-1

Print information available on the last page

Rev. date: 12/08/2020

THE ADVENTURES OF TOMMY AND TINA

Dreaming of Becoming a Loggerhead Sea Turtle and Swimming Down the Treasure Coast

The Story

It was a hot summer day and Tommy and Tina, child friends had been playing all day on the beach and swimming in the ocean. They had fun building sand castles and covering themselves with sand and throwing some snacks in the air and watching the seagulls fly by and catch the snacks in midair and fly away. The ocean was cool on Tommy and Tina's feet as they held hands while jumping the ocean waves. Tommy and Tina liked to watch the little sand crabs crawl back into the sand as the ocean waves rolled across the sand. Tommy and Tina enjoyed collecting a sand bucket full of sea shells and then they held the big sea shells next to their ears, so they could hear the roaring of the ocean in the shell. Tommy and Tina saw some mounds of sand that were protected with small flags and the lifeguard told Tommy and Tina that these mounds were the nesting areas for Loggerhead turtles and the Mother turtle had laid her eggs under the warm sand and soon baby Loggerhead turtles would be hatching and digging their way out from under the sand and crawling back to the ocean to find their mother. Tommy and Tina were getting tired from the hot sun and laid down on their large fluffy beach towel under a big multi-colored beach umbrella to take a nap. Tommy and Tina began to dream about these turtles hatching and Tommy and Tina saw themselves in the dream becoming one of those new born Loggerhead turtles.

Some Information about Loggerhead Turtles

Loggerhead Turtles got their name because they have a large head and a big beak. When they are born they are about 2 1/2 inches long but can grow to over 45 inches long and weigh hundreds of pounds as an adult. Loggerhead Turtles can live for over 50 years. The adult female turtles normally in early summer in tropical climates will crawl from the seashore to the beach and dig a large hole in the dry sand with their flippers and lay hundreds of eggs. Baby turtles will hatch in late summer in the cool of the night. Hatching at night helps avoid predators and the heat of the day. The baby turtles break their shell with their beak and neck and with their flippers they dig their way out of the sand, normally in large groups they crawl to the water. The baby turtles are fair game for the seagulls, crabs, fish and raccoons. The baby grows quickly eating bottom dwelling sea urchins, crushing them with their powerful jaws and soon they grow too large for predators to eat. The baby Loggerhead Turtles have a grey and brown shell and the adult turtles have a reddish brown color. The Loggerhead Turtles are graceful swimmers and live worldwide mostly in warm tropical waters. They travel swimming the ocean waters for 7 to 12 years and then return to live near coastal waters. Loggerhead Turtles are listed on the endangered species act and the National Marine Fisheries Service and the U.S. Fish and Wildlife Services work with other nations to ensure that they are protected.

Tommy And Tina Are Dreaming

In the setting Sun, the mother Loggerhead turtle crawled carefully from the Ocean to the sandy beach to find a nesting place for her turtle eggs. Mother Loggerhead turtle knew not to build the nest too close to the ocean because the waves, during a high tide will wash the turtle eggs back into the ocean. Mother Loggerhead is very smart and finds a good nesting area near the tall green seagrass. Under the cover of darkness avoiding any animals that might like to eat the turtle eggs, Mother Loggerhead turtle digs a hole with her flippers until the hole is deep enough to hold all of her eggs. Mother Loggerhead turtle carefully lays her eggs, one by one, the size of small white balls into the hole during the night. She then very carefully covers the eggs with the silky sand trying hard not to shake the new eggs. Mother Loggerhead turtle then crawls back into the ocean leaving her flipper prints on the beach to be washed away with the incoming ocean waves.

Tommy And Tina Being Born As Loggerhead Sea Turtles

It has been over 2 months since the Mother Loggerhead turtle laid her little turtle eggs in the warm beach sand and the new baby Loggerhead turtles are ready to be born. Tommy and Tina crack open their egg shells under the sand and while wiping the sand from their eyes with their flippers Tommy yells out, "Is that you Tina" and Tina wiping her eyes with her flipper yells out, "Is that you Tommy" yes said Tommy, and it looks like we turned into little Loggerhead turtles, Tina. Let's get out of these shells and crawl back into the ocean and find our mother. Tommy said, we need to wait until it is dark so the seagulls do not eat us before we get back into the ocean, good idea, said Tina. Looks like it is dark enough to run to the ocean now said Tina, let's run fast said Tommy, I see some sea gulls flying nearby. Run Tina, Run Tina, here come the seagulls said Tommy, dive into the ocean Tina said Tommy. Wow that was a close call, said Tommy; I felt a peck from a seagull on my shell. The water tastes a little salty said Tina, because it is salt water said Tommy. Whatever said Tina? Let's look for our mother; there she is talking to Maddie the Mackerel and Ryan and Rod the Red Snappers. Hey Mom yelled Tommy and Tina, we were almost eaten by Seagulls while we were running on the beach, and you are safe now, said mother Loggerhead turtle. Where is our home, said Tina? Follow us into the Indian River lagoon and stay close to Larry the Leatherback Turtle, he is our neighbor and he knows the way, said Mother Loggerhead turtle.

Tommy And Tina Growing Up In The Indian River Lagoon

Tommy and Tina grew quickly as they ate healthy meals every day, their favorite food was the small sea animals like crabs and snails and other sea urchins that lived in the river grasses. Tommy and Tina met many friends as they grew to adult turtles; they met Audrey the pretty angel fish with her two babies Allison and Jeff. Tommy and Tina had a few scary friends like Alex the baby alligator and Evan and Erin the electric eels. They all played in the seagrass and the warm waters of the lagoon. One morning they were swimming around the rocks and met Hannah the Hog fish and Kyle the king fish and lying on the sand was Sydney the squid. Be careful, Sydney the squid likes to grab you with her long arms said Kyle the kingfish. Hannah the Hogfish chewing some sea grass said, what are your names? We are Tommy and Tina the Loggerhead turtles. Why do they call you Loggerhead turtles asked Kyle the talking kingfish, because we have very large heads and strong jaws said Tommy, that's cool said Sydney the squid. I am glad we are all friends and play nice together but be carefully of Kelly the crab, she likes to bite you just for fun, it is like a little kiss that pinches, said Sydney the Squid.

Tommy And Tina Swim To The Ocean To Meet New Friends

Hey Tommy yelled Tina the Loggerhead turtle, I think we are old enough to go out into the ocean and meet some new friends, good idea Tina said Tommy but we need to be careful because the fish are bigger and the waves are stronger. The water feels a little cooler than the water in the river said Tina, stop acting like a baby turtle, said Tommy the water feels refreshing. Hey Tommy look at all of these fish coming to look at us, said Tina, I hope they are friendly fish and do not want to eat us for dinner, some of them are pretty large. Hey Tommy and Tina yelled out the fish, we have swum over to meet you, your mother told us you would be swimming in the Ocean today. What are your names said Tina, my name is Linda the Lionfish and this is the shark family, Sid and Sandy and baby Sheila the shark sucker, over here is Lisa the lizardfish, Tom the Toadfish, Mike and Michelle the monkfish and Gretchen and Kent the groupers. Here comes Mackie and Maddie the mackerels said Linda the lionfish. Thanks for coming to meet us said Tina the turtle, you all look so different in size, in shape and in color, how did you all become friends? It took many years of learning about each other before we finally figured it out, said Maddie the mackerel. It was a lot better for all of us, if we were all friends and helped each other live in this large ocean. There are plenty more fish friends to meet said Maddie the mackerel, swim over into the deeper water and meet some more ocean friends.

Tommy And Tina Swim Over To See
The Treasure Chest

Hey Tina gurgled Tommy, let's swim over and see what the other fish are looking at in the deeper water. Look Tina said Tommy all of the fish are swimming around that old wooden chest. I wonder what they are talking about. Hey Tommy and Tina gurgled Dennis the doctor fish, swim over here and look at the sunken wooden treasure chest and meet a few new friends. We are Tommy and Tina the Loggerhead turtles; good to meet you said Professor the pigfish and pugs the pastor pinfish and fly the funny flounder. Wow thanks for coming over to meet us said Tina the turtle. What do you think was in this old wooden box said Tommy. I think it was some gold and jewelry that was lost at sea many years ago said George and Gail the gag fish. How did you know that said Cathy the clownfish, because it is old and rusted and here is a gold coin said Chet the catfish and Patsy the red porgy? Let's try to open the box said Joe the jackknife fish. Look there is a gold coin at the bottom of the box said Richard the redfish. I bet there are many more gold coins and jewelry here on the treasure coast said Ann the amberjack. Tommy and Tina yelled out, wiggle your tail if you want to swim down the treasure coast and look for gold and jewelry. If we swim in a school we will be safe from Willy the wale, let's get Bob the Barracuda and Debbie the Dolphin to show us the way. All of the fish wiggled their tails and yelled out; we are all excited, what a fun Idea. Let's start swimming said Cathy the Clownfish we have a lot of fun things to see.

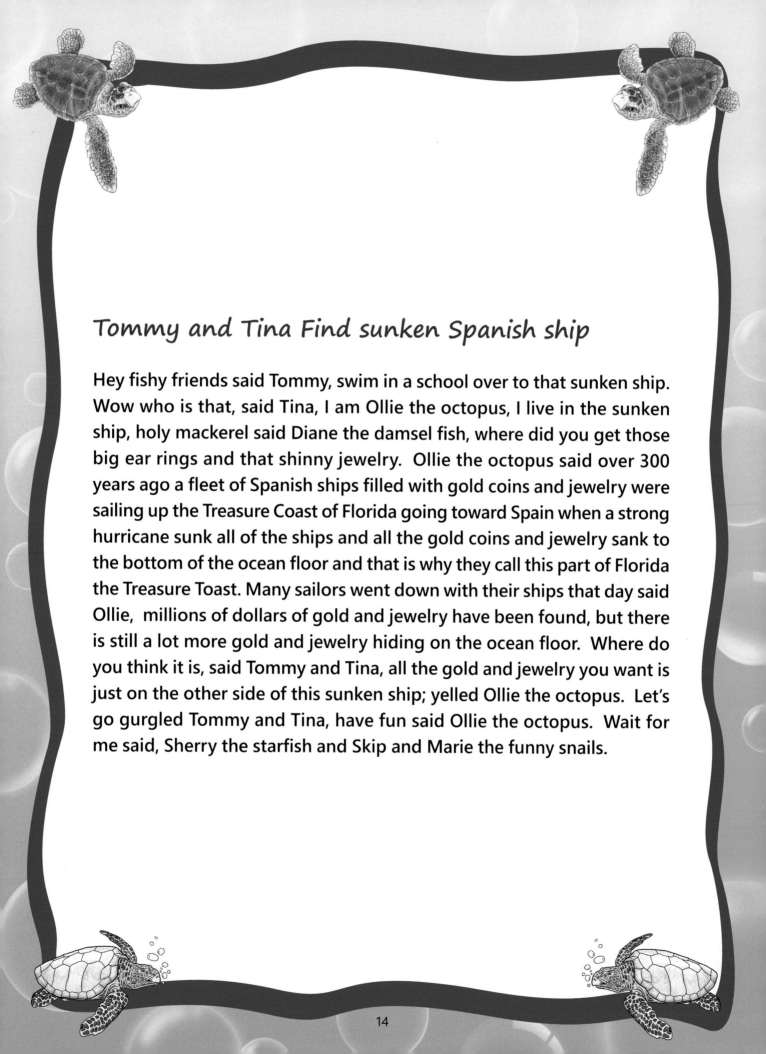

Tommy and Tina Find sunken Spanish ship

Hey fishy friends said Tommy, swim in a school over to that sunken ship. Wow who is that, said Tina, I am Ollie the octopus, I live in the sunken ship, holy mackerel said Diane the damsel fish, where did you get those big ear rings and that shinny jewelry. Ollie the octopus said over 300 years ago a fleet of Spanish ships filled with gold coins and jewelry were sailing up the Treasure Coast of Florida going toward Spain when a strong hurricane sunk all of the ships and all the gold coins and jewelry sank to the bottom of the ocean floor and that is why they call this part of Florida the Treasure Toast. Many sailors went down with their ships that day said Ollie, millions of dollars of gold and jewelry have been found, but there is still a lot more gold and jewelry hiding on the ocean floor. Where do you think it is, said Tommy and Tina, all the gold and jewelry you want is just on the other side of this sunken ship; yelled Ollie the octopus. Let's go gurgled Tommy and Tina, have fun said Ollie the octopus. Wait for me said, Sherry the starfish and Skip and Marie the funny snails.

Tommy And Tina Find Gold And Jewelry By The Sunken Ship

Wow look at all these gold coins and jewelry, said Tina. It must be our lucky day, because there is Kim the cool horseshoe crab sitting on top of a box of gold jewelry. Come on fishy friends let's do a dress up and put on some of this jewelry. Look, Mackie the mackerel looks like a girl with those large ear rings and Chet the catfish looks funny with the nose ring, look there is Linda the lion fish and Gretchen the grouper and fly the flounder all wearing belly button rings. I always thought fly the flounder was a bit different said Captain Dave and Mel the mate yelling from the sunken ship. Who are you guys yelled Kim the horseshoe crab, we are the ghosts of the sunken ship said Captain Dave. You guys are a little scary looking, said Kathleen the baby eel. Oh no, it is Tom the toadfish and Norman the native stargazer wearing a neckless around their tail fins, what a funny sight to see, said Linda the lionfish. This is a lot of fun my fishy friends, yelled Tommy and Tina, but we need to leave the jewelry and be on our way swimming down the Treasure Coast, we still have a few more miles to swim to the end of the Treasure Coast. How will we know when we are at the end of the Treasure Coast yelled Ronnie the roaming sheep head fish. Tommy gurgled we will see the Jupiter light house which marks the beginning of the Palm Coast and the end of the Treasure Coast and the end of our adventure. I hope there is some soft sand to rest on at the Jupiter lighthouse, I am starting to get tired yelled Erin the electric eel. Let's get swimming yelled Tommy before Erin falls asleep.

Tommy And Tina And Their Fishy Friends Swim Past The St Lucie Power Plant

Hey Tommy, yelled Tina, I think the water is getting warmer, you are right said Tommy we are getting close to the St Lucie Power Plant. The Power Plant sucks in water from the ocean and uses the cool water to help generate electric power to light thousands of homes here on the Treasure Coast said Tommy. What makes the water warm said Tina, the water cools down the hot generators and then the warm water flows back into the ocean. Can the water hurt you, said Tina? Some fish say it can make you glow, wow said Tina, how does it feel to be glowing? I think you get a warm fuzzy feeling, said Lu Lu the little spot fish. The warm water is a favorite fishing spot for many fishermen, look there is Al, Dick and True the anglers, be careful fishy friends they will try to catch you and eat you for dinner, said Tommy. I will stop that said Erin and Ed the electric eels and Nancy the naughty perch, let's swim over and knock their bait off their hooks, they will never know their bait is missing said Rod the red snapper, all they do is drink beer and tell funny stories all day.

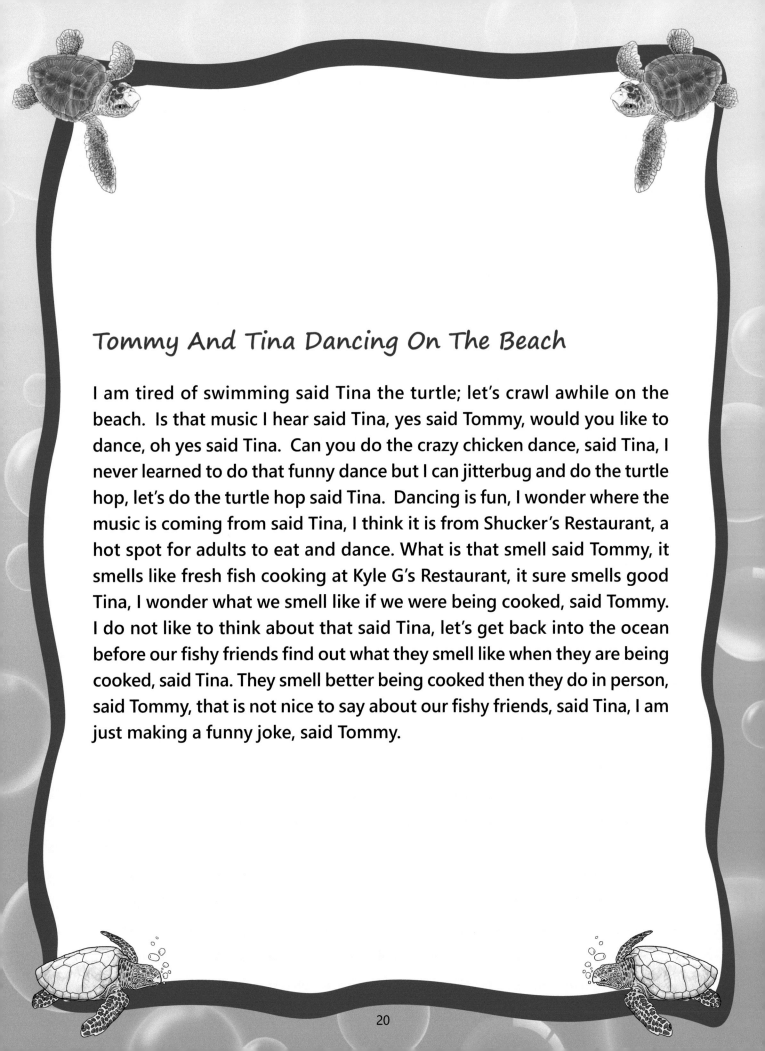

Tommy And Tina Dancing On The Beach

I am tired of swimming said Tina the turtle; let's crawl awhile on the beach. Is that music I hear said Tina, yes said Tommy, would you like to dance, oh yes said Tina. Can you do the crazy chicken dance, said Tina, I never learned to do that funny dance but I can jitterbug and do the turtle hop, let's do the turtle hop said Tina. Dancing is fun, I wonder where the music is coming from said Tina, I think it is from Shucker's Restaurant, a hot spot for adults to eat and dance. What is that smell said Tommy, it smells like fresh fish cooking at Kyle G's Restaurant, it sure smells good Tina, I wonder what we smell like if we were being cooked, said Tommy. I do not like to think about that said Tina, let's get back into the ocean before our fishy friends find out what they smell like when they are being cooked, said Tina. They smell better being cooked then they do in person, said Tommy, that is not nice to say about our fishy friends, said Tina, I am just making a funny joke, said Tommy.

Tommy And Tina Swimming Past
The Port St Lucie Inlet And Arriving At
The Jupiter Lighthouse

Tommy and Tina swimming, Tommy says to Tina, look that is sailfish point, we are crossing the Port St Lucie Inlet; swim hard fishy friends the current in the inlet is strong sometimes and be careful of the boats speeding out into the ocean, their propellers could hurt you. Wow there goes Uncle Dave and Aunt Pat speeding in their race boat, lets wave said Tina, they do not know we are turtles said Tommy. I forgot we were turtles said Tina. Look there is Jupiter rocks, said Vance and Ryder the Twin Pompano's; we must be getting close to Jupiter Light house. I am glad said Jules the jelly fish, and Bobby the Baby Marlin, I am getting tired of swimming. Hey Tina said Tommy look at all those fish at the Jupiter inlet, I think it is our welcome committee said, Tommy and Tina. Welcome to the Jupiter lighthouse said Bruce, Barbara and Brenda the blowfish, we got together some local fish friends to greet you, say hi to Scotty the Snook, Chris the Cobia, Butch the black Drum, Ted the Tuna, Jimmy the Jackfish and Tammy the Tripletail. Thanks for swimming over to greet us, we had a very exciting journey down the Treasure Coast said Tommy and Tina. We were all glad to see the Jupiter Lighthouse, it guided us thru the dark ocean waters at night, the same way it has guided many boats home from the ocean. We are all very tired and need to get some sleep, we will tell you our story tomorrow before we leave to swim home. Good night fishy friends, we had a fun journey, get a good night sleep and don't forget to say your good night prayers, we have a lot to be thankful for, goodnight, sweet dreams.

Printed in the United States
By Bookmasters